Seeds of G

by

Briony Davies

A basic guide for teachers and others to enable lessons based on ecosystems to be enlivened.
The school grounds should be seen as a huge asset worthy of serious investment for future generations.

First Edition January 2011

Written in the year of
Biodiversity 2010

With the assistance of friends and associates
to whom I extend my gratitude.

© briony davies

All rights reserved. No part of this publication may be reproduced, stored in a retrieval system or transmitted in any form or by any means, electronic, mechanical, photocopying, recording or otherwise, without prior permission of the publisher,

ISBN 978-0-9568444-0-8

Published by seeds of green.co.uk
Printed by Gomer Press Ltd

Contents

Introducing 'Seeds of Green

"Life in sunshine or in rain, is beautiful",

Arthur Mee, editor of the Children's Newspaper, 1952

Today's children are tomorrow's environmental protectors. The school landscape and its care can give young people a sense of belonging and stewardship which should be encouraged; a blank play area leaves them with a negative attitude to the natural environment.

Interacting with nature seems so alien, so distant and so scary. How can we address this problem?

How can we recreate a bit of wilderness that we can keep control of?

-That will survive a hoard of children yet still serve its purpose?

Developing the school surroundings to even the smallest degree, by planting to encourage wildlife to share the spare space, will build up a relationship between the youngsters and the other inhabitants of their world. Seeing birds feeding on fruit and aphids amongst the plants, that can easily be grown, will invite interaction and curiosity; which in turn will lead to their social, physical and mental heightened awareness. Also, using their senses to listen to bird song; training their eyes to seek fine detail and movement, and at the same time to observe colour and texture; will all add to the rounding-out of their character.

Grey Wagtail

-- a little bird that is fond of water and eats small insects which it catches in mountain streams; they are related to the Pied Wagtail which is a frequent resident in towns.

"Nature-deficit disorder" is a phrase coined by Richard Louv in his reaction to hyperactivity. Research has shown decisively that children who have problems when they are confined indoors are relatively free of them after working outside. Nature's wonder and complexity allows young people to feel part of the overall scheme for the world to which they belong and in which almost everything they do plays a crucial part. The element of discovery in nature provides a stimulus to the imagination that no other medium can provide. The space provided by the environment in all its moods is incredibly important for practicing good behaviour and self discipline, in contrast to the inflexibility of the confines of a building.

As with human communication and the daily ritual of living, we need rhythm and occasional tuning for the contrasts of peace and excitement to be fully enjoyed. Consequently foresight and ingenuity and a confident knowledgeable attitude are among the attributes needed to create schemes with natural things and to harmonize these with architecture and civil engineering.

Times are changing and we have to face the challenge and assist nature to participate in our future.

The history of landscape began with us facing 'brutal' nature and battling to overcome the encroaching forest and wilderness – now is the turning point.

We have beaten back the forest and tamed the wild beasts – indeed nearly exterminated them.

Now is the time that we need to integrate nature into our lives and for architects to appreciate that harmony between the built environment and the things of the earth is essential to the future well-being of the planet.

The wild stallion with no shelter!

Here our attempts to recreate forest has become a blot on the landscape that is host to very few creatures indeed, despite the fact that it could be there for forty years before felling.

Young people are building body and muscle when they run around outside, and their instinct is to do just that. Once they have released their energy and their brains are reinvigorated by the increased oxygen, they will apply their **brainpower** in the classroom.

On Earth increasing plant density for oxygen production is necessary, now more than ever, if it is not to end up resembling that 'green cheese' in the sky – mouldy and desolate and totally inhospitable. It may seem an over simplified question, but why do astronauts take oxygen to the Moon? Because there is no plant life there.

The school grounds should be seen by the management as a huge and valuable asset that is worthy of serious **investment**.

A design should not be inhibited by the idea that the children will automatically feel a destructive urge - the best way to counteract this is to involve as many children as possible in the design and construction process. It is the odd one out; the one who feels hard done by or has not been consulted, who will feel aggrieved and will cause a problem. A small task allocated to each youngster should reduce any animosity later.

This construction was deemed too dangerous and demolished ! ! !

The children had no vote.

A magnificent setting but WHY so much fencing? WHY so much unutilised grass and no hedge? So much cutting to do! Such a feeling of exposure and insecurity.

Why not plant a winter flowering Viburnam 'Eve Price' *hedge?*

Many grounds are blank and uninteresting and this leaves the youngsters with a negative attitude to the natural environment and the outdoors generally. Classroom planning ahead, for a venture outdoors, should ensure that the children are focused and enthusiastic about the chosen subject so that full use is made of time outside. The problem with 'attitudes' is that the children will go outside with the thought of 'play' on their minds; the challenge is to provide them with a subject that will engage them fully and encourage their dedication.

Learning to plant trees and other plants whether for ornament, for wildlife or for eating is a good start for youngsters, but their enthusiasm needs to be sustained with variety. They need to learn that local birds need insects and that mammals need places to hide and that all these rely on the eco-system that we all share. Their needs includes plenty of food availability, together with sufficient space and habitat variety; with a huge diversity of plants all combined in one great mix. Nature offers endless opportunities for children to investigate matters within their other lessons: the complexity of **food webs** in woodlands; the planting of a staple crop, and the examination of some of the teeming world of 80 million species of invertebrates; leading to the designing and planning of their own nature trails to accommodate as many of these facets as possible.

This 'mess' is the abandoned home of a tunnel spider; it is overloaded with the remains of beetles and flies and anything tasty that came her way.

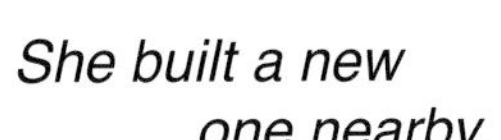

She built a new one nearby.

Is this what we want? destructive farming . . . . .

If this generation doesn't embrace ecological gardening and organic farming, there is little hope for their future, because we humans have proliferated beyond the carrying capacity of the earth and our excessive consumption is having an unprecedented impact on our planet.

Annual **rainfall** in England and Wales is at its lowest since records began in 1767. Britain also has the lowest tree cover in the whole of Europe [see w3 Midland Forest]. We are very capable of destroying ourselves and the introvert feeling fostered by this knowledge is what Geoffrey Jellicoe, the great landscape architect, suggests we must avoid: "the urge to go back to the uniformity of our cell. . . . . because . . . . . it is still awe-inspiring to reflect that even in the modern world we should all perish within a few days if nature failed to be fertile".

We are going ever upward without considering the importance of what is left: here the wrong plants have been used around the buildings, and have been planted too close together so have then had to be cut back. The planting is useless to wildlife; aesthetically displeasing; impractical.

Landscape versus architecture?

The architect, Corbusier designed upward to permit space to be released for more people-friendly activity and landscaping, but he was misinterpreted! Even Frank Lloyd Wright the builder of 'Falling Water' said that, "The best friend of man is the tree. When we use the tree respectfully and economically, we have one of the greatest resources on the earth".

The building materials we take for granted come from or are derived from the depths of the earth's crust; but, in contrast to this, plant material only grows on the lit surface of the earth or sea and is dependent on precipitation for survival. The variations in the earth's surface are many and diverse and man's interference with them creates even more problematic consequences than nature itself: understanding the 'spirit of the place' can lead to endless opportunities for designing with nature.

Plant communities can be easily seen in Limestone pavement or from planting a lot of seeds together to see which like the soil, etc.

Limestone pavement, here with exposed crevices that are usually colonized by plants.

In the 1930's in response to the proliferation of the use of concrete and large expanses of tarmac the Roads Beautifying Association was set up but it soon became obvious that it was not possible to achieve aesthetically pleasing landscape as readily as building a three-lane road. Trees take time to establish and they have to acclimatise to new surroundings too. Man can very quickly alter his surroundings, but it takes nature far longer to repair the scars.

There is a great need for more planting of complete communities rather than just trees on their own. Study of the plants' habits and needs, combined with forethought is needed to avoid disasters as the plants mature.

Blending compatible plants, here Bugle and Ferns, that are suitable for the situation will result in a planting scheme which will look and feel natural and be pleasing to the eye.

7 Planning: a key to success

A long-term plan is essential; it will save time, money, effort and a lot of patience. Slowly… slowly… is the best way to progress, and the plan also needs to allow for some permanencies and some things of a temporary nature. The reason for this is, obviously, that every year there is a new intake of pupils and if there is an overall plan they will be able to get involved by re-doing what the previous year tried their hand at. Another reason could be to spread out the finances over the long term. A fast approach to satisfy a 'must have now' attitude can lead to a great deal of unnecessary maintenance and this should be avoided at all costs for it can lead to disillusionment.

This great leap forward into the world outside the classroom could be quite daunting.

Why not consider having an **eco-manager** who could be an expert in either natural history or landscaping, at least someone who would be willing and able to bring in and co-ordinate other experts like botanists or craftspeople. If one eco-manager could cover three or more schools in a county that would be ideal. They could also instigate **Garden Clubs**.

As the teachers will have preparatory work to do regarding the change from an indoor teaching situation, to a sometimes alien and completely different environment outdoors, the involvement of a coordinator is imperative. Assessing what will be needed and preparing for the outdoor lesson will have to be agreed between teacher and manager if everything is to go smoothly and safely. The management will involve working out timetables on a daily and yearly basis, while also fitting in with the seasonal changes and the **curriculum**. Finally there is the small matter of ensuring that the planting year coincides with the academic year.

A wild, acid soil, sward with a balanced mix of fine grasses and wild flowers. This is in Charnwood forest in Leicestershire a site of special scientific interest, known as an SSSI. A useful kind of place for a study visit.

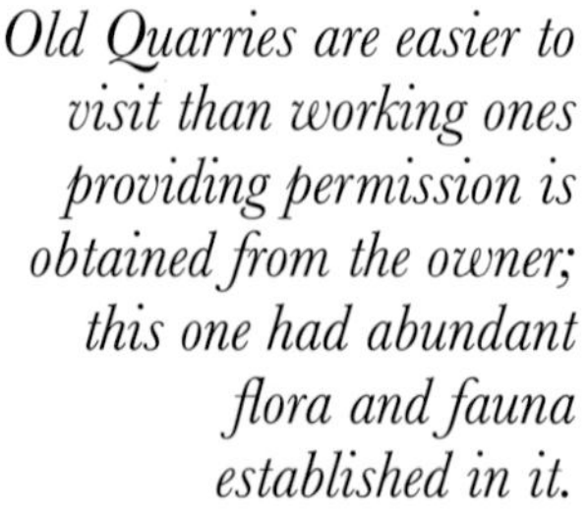

Old Quarries are easier to visit than working ones providing permission is obtained from the owner; this one had abundant flora and fauna established in it.

Survey

Surveying the whole site first has the advantage of being an exercise in observation and also in measuring; the details in this can be relevant to Geography; Geology; Art; Biology; Environmental Studies; Maths and many other subjects.

The above is the hole to a mason bee nest in the old lime mortar of a brick wall.

In the appendices is a sample survey sheet that can be laid out to suit the needs of the teacher and when completed can provide a list of useful facts that can be adapted in the classroom as part of lessons. This can be extended to include boundary heights; the buildings and their details.

Even the smallest detail can be recorded for the survey. This is a lesson in observation and a first step towards inspiration and curiosity which can quicken the mind in the classroom.

This picture may at first appear somewhat boring and not in the least bit artistic but it illustrates several factors to be considered in a survey. First it tells you which direction you are looking in due to the shadows. Next observe the water pipe and note that it is not protected from frost in the winter. The wall has several features to look for, one: has it got mortar holding it together or is it dry stone work? What is the plant that the man is picking fruit off? It is a **grape vine** and it is trained over a shade pergola and he is picking the fruit to press for the juice.
In the distance there is a high pole with an old barrel fixed on it out of the way of predators; what is it used by?
Finally what species of tree is in the distance and what indicates the season of the year?

One further observation could be a description of the grass sward and leaves taken for identification using a hand lens. All this information can be used for compiling project books.

The survey could also involve some pupils in sketching details; especially of layout; stone wall building; structure outlines; any special features on site, and then what is beyond the boundaries that is visible. Video and photographs should not be included until the next stage to maximise the observation techniques and fully assess proportions and sensual feel of leaves and stone and bark etc. This will add art in the form of sketches and written descriptions for use later. Observation of textures, colours and sizes will all be useful for other lessons.

Planning for vegetables

Potatoes: several kinds nearly at flowering stage

Space for vegetables should take into account the consideration that each year four beds will be needed per class. This is very important for vegetables, for long term use. It is no good trying to give each student four sections each: it will take up too much space and there will be difficulty with continuity. Lessons in **rotational** planting are very important; Root Crops and Legumes need to be moved annually. Onions can go in the same place each year, but are usually slotted into the rotation for convenience. A fourth bed can also be used for demonstrating **green manuring**.

These Peas have been trained on a daily basis to reach 8' or over 2 meters high. This represents dedication to a task. This is known as the 90-day Pea because it can be eaten 90 days from planting.

Peas and beans and other Legumes are nitrogen fixing – they have bacterial nodes on the roots which put nutrition back into the soil: hence their value in a rotation. These nodules can be observed easily in clover at any time of the year.

Broad Beans fit into the school terms well because they can be started in the winter, after new year, and will be ready for eating first as a young whole pod.

Raised beds: these are not essential, however it may be advantageous to use them to provide a better drained growing place if the site is wet or heavy clay or over acidic. The height is important, as above about 30 cm will dry out too much. The position needs to be as sunny as possible and too much shade should be avoided; though if the shade is only at mid day this will be suitable. They should not be more than 2m wide for small people and 3m for older ones.

Land form:
Almost invariably a school grounds will have been flattened when the school was built. By planning ahead for changes a major contribution to the excitement of the future design will be made by investing in some shaping with a machine. One good man with an excavator can easily transform the site into useful contours. Adding an **amphitheatre** or using a corner to make terraces will allow lessons and performances to take place.

Tarmac

The most familiar surface and the most unfriendly, can be a lesson on its own. The tar has been extracted from under the ground (or sea) and transported many miles and it is mixed with crushed rock that has been quarried out of the ground. what more uncompromising surface could children be expected to play on? Because it is generally black it absorbs the heat of the sun and can revert to sticky stuff. Given time, nature can take over and mosses establish during the winter season. This can be speeded up if weeds at the edge of the tarmac have been had weedkiller applied. Why?

These interesting processes are what botanists refer to as the pioneer invasion. They begin with mosses and then progressively create conditions ripe for the higher plants: alpines and dry ground species followed by shrubs and then ultimately trees.

Existing **tarmac**:There is no need to destroy all that has been inherited.
Taking the whole lot up would be an expensive and unnecessary expense, especially if the tarmac is in good condition. However, old tarmac that is beginning to crumble is another matter. There are ways of dealing with it. If it is slightly broken up to allow free drainage, raised beds can be placed on top of it. Old turf placed upside down in the bottom will give them a moisture-retentive start under the new soil. Another way is to mark out paths and dig holes where planting is to take place. New soil can be put in the hole as long as there is not a solid barrier to roots underneath the tarmac. The paths can then have an alternative surface of bark or gravel put over it (preferably not wood chips). A cutting machine can be used to cut large patterns if necessary.

Techno-help

Future plans could include the siting of a CCTV; night vision would be interesting; to observe and record wildlife visitors to bird boxes or roof gardens, or to the pond. They can be used inside a bird box.

Rainwater from the existing buildings should be considered for use in the landscape or vegetable garden. Ingenious ways of directing it to where it is needed could be devised; it could flow through a raised pool before going somewhere else, via a bog garden; it could be raised up using a solar panel; it could be used for water wheels; fountains, all sorts of things! Rainwater traps can be fixed to the existing down pipe.

A roof pond: a safe place for birds to drink, but not in full sun to avoid drying out.

CONCRETE has its place.
Concrete rings come in various sizes and two regular shapes which are fairly easy for two people to manoeuvre, but should a small machine be available these could be stacked up, to be used for planting, climbing, or incorporating into earth banks, using a bit of ingenuity. They can be filled with earth or hardcore, with turf upside down on top but for soil a layer of drainage material will be needed in the bottom few centimetres. If they are used singly for planting, the concrete lends itself to being surfaced as a project, using mosaics or dry stone walling or painting plants on. Rectangular ones come in approx. 10 cm depth and can be built to any reasonable height and won't need a machine to stack. Their usefulness is that each class can have some each. As planting beds they shouldn't be too high for vegetables because they will dry out too easily; unless, that is, you are growing long show carrots! They are not expensive and are robust and easily available.

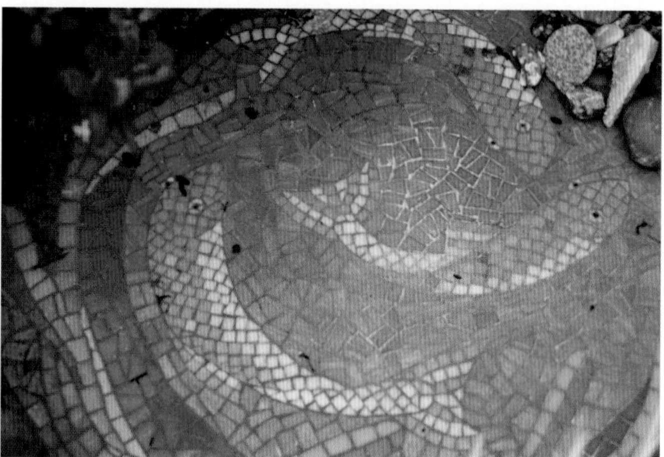

Good **leadership** is key to the success of such a scheme. Someone who will take advice from professionals and be capable of clear decision making for the benefit of the pupils. Someone who has vision and a basic knowledge of landscape design and/or planning.

FENCING

Too solid. But a brick base for a fence is a good idea.

Fencing of solid wood structure is not the best form of barrier next to any planting area, nor playing area for that matter, this is simply because when the wind blows a turbulent down draft is created on the far side of it; this applies to high walls as well.

If it must be used, then an alternative building pattern, using alternate planks on each side to create an open gap in-between, will bring the wind pressure down.

Oliver Rackham, in 'History of the Countryside' (1986), (p.25) remembered the landscape of his childhood, though richer than now, as already suffering from what Prof. Babington, an earlier botanist, described as the 'loss' of four things:
"There is the loss of beauty, especially that exquisite beauty of the small and complex and unexpected, of Frog Orchids, of Sundews or of Dragonflies. There is the loss of freedom, of highways and open spaces. . . . . . There is the loss of historic vegetation and wildlife, most of which has gone forever. . . . . I am especially concerned with the loss of meaning. The landscape is a record of our roots and the growth of **civilisation**".

Aesthetics, what aesthetics?

The boundaries of existing schools in modern premises are likely to consist of a mixture of steel fencing, though of old walls in older ones. These modern defensive or protective barriers or 'cages' are quick to erect with all too easily obtainable, often, man made materials whose making hides the cost to the environment of production!

The landscape of our ancestors who lived on the hills amongst the Oak and Ash wooded vegetation.

Harebells and Thistles regrowing after sheep have been grazed. This will return to scrub and then woodland if left alone.

Hedges

What choice of environmentally friendly boundaries are there? What materials are used locally? Are there traditional methods still in use that speak of local character? There are hedges and walls. Despite many hundreds of miles of hedges being grubbed out, along with their inhabitants, in recent decades, most British counties still have some. They are not expensive to establish and then only need one annual cut in the winter.

This is a hawthorn hedge that has been planted for ten-to-fifteen years and then carefully cut and laid in the traditional way to provide a very strong and impenetrable barrier, and hopefully a new home for wildlife at the same time.

If a thorny hedge is seen as problematic then Field Maple can be used, especially on limestone soil, mixed with other native species.

After laying, because hedgeing people prefer a single species initially, other plants can be added to increase the bio-diversity value of the boundary: such as Field rose, *Rosa arvensis; Rosa canina*; Honeysuckle; Wild Privet, and **Holly**. These can be planted as plugs which the children can have grown! Or they can be purchased as single-stem and bare-root plants a year old. A full mixed planting of up to 12 species would be suitable if it fits into the scheme of things. The base of the hedge is where many dry-ground wildflowers will grow, including Primroses; Wood Betony and Cowslips. A dense growth of these is as important as the hedge itself.

Usually hedge laying is done after the leaves have fallen off the deciduous species but with climate change this is getting later and later in the year. Here a very happy hedging man who has competed in early Autumn. Hedging competitions are held every year - no one gets paid for this! There are different styles in other areas of the country.

As this task will only need to be done every 50 or so years it would be a good idea to make a **video** of this special event so that future pupils will be able to see how it was done. The age of an existing hedge can sometimes be determined by counting the numbers of species it contains: from the guideline that a mature hedge adds one more species naturally every 100 years. Hedges clothe the boundaries and furnish them as an interesting background of immense value, but most importantly provides a coherent and sheltered route around the grounds for wildlife. Birds will make use of the cover for their **fledglings**; to shelter them from predators and provide some seclusion.

Country crafts feature in art, poetry and English literature: **Shakespeare**, a native of Warwickshire, mentions in Hamlet: “There is a divinity that shapes mens ends, hew them as we will”, a reference to shaping and hewing the hedges with a cleaver.

This is a cleft-wood gate that could have been made from the wood out of the hedge, usually Hazel wood, sometimes Ash or Chestnut; while Oak would be kept for gate posts. Where there is no stone available the hedge was planted on top of an earth bank but in stony country it would be clad in stone: see below.

Walls

This is a typical Welsh 'clawdd': a very old example, similar boundaries can be seen in Cornwall. A ditch was created by piling excavated clay inside the wall, which then acted as a drain for the field. Sometimes the boulders were joined by sods of earth in between them. 'Clawdd' usually ended up being clothed in grass for the sheep to graze; with the hedge planted on top out of their reach. Ditches provide valuable sheltered hollows for creatures when and where there are adverse weather conditions.

Dry-stone walls are found up and down Britain from Scotland to Devon; in Derbyshire in Yorkshire and Cumbria.

This wall was not intended to be pleasing to the eye; it was intended as a boundary on the mountain; but pleasing it is.

Children love having a go at this craft; they find it hard to believe that it can be achieved without mortar. And yet a whole house can be built this way. Later buildings had limestone mortar between the stones with lime-mortar wall-rendering inside where once clay would have been used. Historically this links in with the lath and plaster in old buildings; a subject for study! A raised bed could be built using this method, as an example, and planted up with wild flowers or Blueberries or both. It provides homes for small mammals.

Turf

SPORTS FIELDS

Sport is an essential activity for youngsters; one aspect of which could be turned to good use by introducing a study of the turf that is such a vital alternative to the pleasures derived from creating mud. The craft of the 'green keeper' is very specialised and completely in opposition to those wishing to create natural vegetation. However, this should not be a problem if everyone appreciates the other's point of view. The official groundsman can be brought on board by his involvement in explaining his work to the pupils and his assistance in identifying the tough turf species of grass that are important for playing football and rugby.

The youngsters soon spotted the purple base of the Rye grass and looked for the seeds, hairs and ligule.

A useful exercise would be to fence off a trial area, only a square meter will do, so that the pupils can identify the species by their flowers in the late Spring, about May/June. The most important species, now much hybridized, is **Rye grass** and can generally be identified from its base growth; with only one other species anything like it and that is Cocksfoot; while another feature is that it is has very shiny leaves. Other species that will be involved in a sward are the species with running root systems that bind the soil in-between the Rye grass. Another interesting design of grass, though not found on a sports field, is the Wild Oat: this has long twisted awns that act as an hygrometer that cause the seed to 'walk'.

Unless the grounds have been especially prepared for sports the chances are that there will be a mixed-meadow sward i.e. some modern breeds of grass in with 'weed' species. There will usually be kinds that are adapted to the ground conditions and soil kind. So Creeping Buttercup or Bog Pimpernel will indicate poorly drained ground and finer leaved grasses and Hawkweeds will be on drier acidic ground.

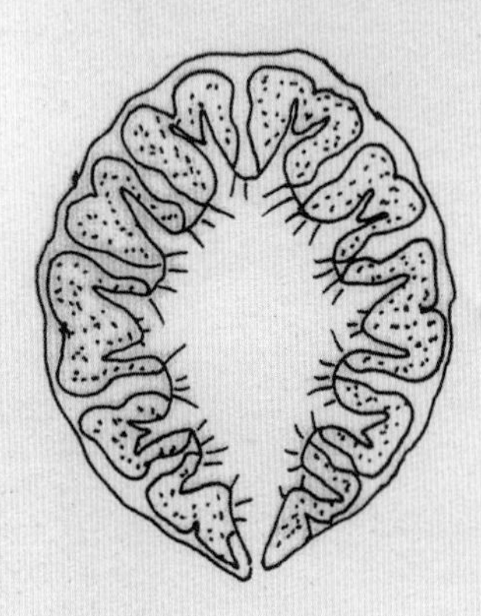

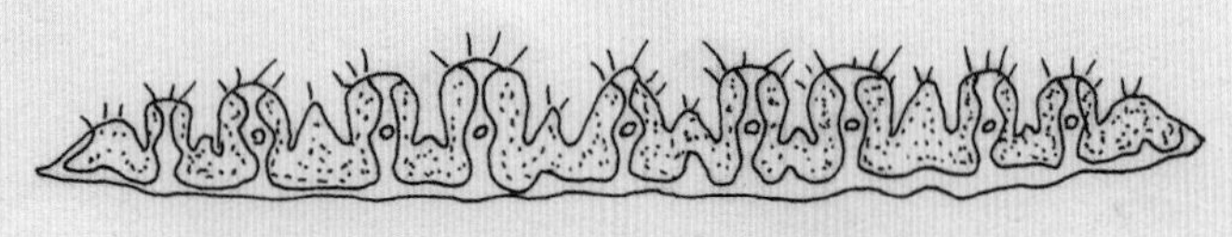

A grass leaf closed, above, in hot, dry conditions;
open in wet weather, left.

Wildflowers

Having sparked off some interest in growing things, move on to inspiring an interest in herbs because these can be introduced on a bank away from the rough and tumble of football: some of them being easy plants to establish with other wild flowers. Below is Bastard Balm, a hedgerow plant that is easy from seed, with Artemisia behind it. The seedling-suppressant around these is spent hops from a brewery. Most of the Compositae family are fairly large-growing plants not found in grassland, often on waste ground and unkempt places, so are easy to identify, as starter plants for lessons in Botany and Art. They include some beautiful Thistles and Campanulas and Hawkweeds, and Dandelion and Burdock to make a brew!

Melittis melissophyllum a wild flower of dry hedge banks a good companion for this is the lovely Wood Betony.

Large Skipper with Marsh Birdsfoot Trefoil

Fewer species grow on acid soil, which will not be useful for playing any games on. This is because they are very slow growing species with fine leaves that often curl up to prevent dessication by the sun and wind. To illustrate to pupils and for them to experiment it would be useful to create a raised bed with a peat mixture. **Vacciniums** and Heathers, planted as **plug** grown young plants, will establish and the Blueberries will produce edible fruit in time. An easy way to check the acidity would be to purchase a simple soil testing kit from a garden shop or an educational supply company. Alternatively a local Horticultural College might oblige.

Carline thistle seed heads; a plant of calcareous soil, amongst fine, specially adapted short grasses as on previous page

Practical study areas

Roz, looking for butterflies

If space is not a problem then cutting a swathe through the grass while leaving a free-growing margin will enable the meadow wildflowers to flourish and the difference between this and the short-cut grass can be observed. Most of the long grass will only need to be cut once a year in the late autumn to spring, leaving some flowerheads for the birds or reseeding. The width of the path and the design of the plot can be altered occasionally.

Creatures like Slow Worms and Frogs enjoy the coolness of long grass in the summer but will retreat to hibernate in dry stone walls and hedges in the winter. Leaving too much area of long grass make it more difficult to explore for research purposes, so long strips are the most practical.

To help the study of all plants the first lesson in Botany could be about Families. For example the **Buttercup** Family includes a running-rhizomed one, a bulbous one and a tall spindly one that only grows in old meadows, where cows ignore it, because it is poisonous to them until it is dried in hay.

Dark Green Fritillary

To create a wild meadow from scratch necessitates removing the rich top soil because wildflowers grow most competitively in soil with very low nutrients. This could be an area that has had the old tarmac removed. The resulting soil could be used for vegetables.

Primula elatior *the true Oxlip a rare member of the primrose family with which it hybridizes. A woodlander that prefers semi shade by a hedgerow.*

There are three things that can be done next. The bare earth can be left for six weeks to see what seeds have survived from previous deposits; this can be quite a surprising exercise. The exposed soil left can be tested for its acidity or alkalinity. Plugs of wildflowers can be planted: these are seedlings grown in a tube ready for planting and are readily obtainable. Otherwise seeds can be planted; but this can be problematic in the school situation as they need careful looking after until established. Children could each have their own plot for experimenting and recording, but pathways would need designing into this scheme to make it practical, which would use up valuable space. **Bark** (not wood chips) over gravel drainage is best for surfacing the paths if these are necessary. Finances permitting 50 cm square concrete slabs are the ideal dividing surface.

Heather growing on dry acid soil
Spot the butterflies!

Below is an example of the wonders of nature; a pair of butterflies photographed on wild heather.

WHO designed these butterflies so that they exactly blended with the heather when they are at their most vulnerable to predation?

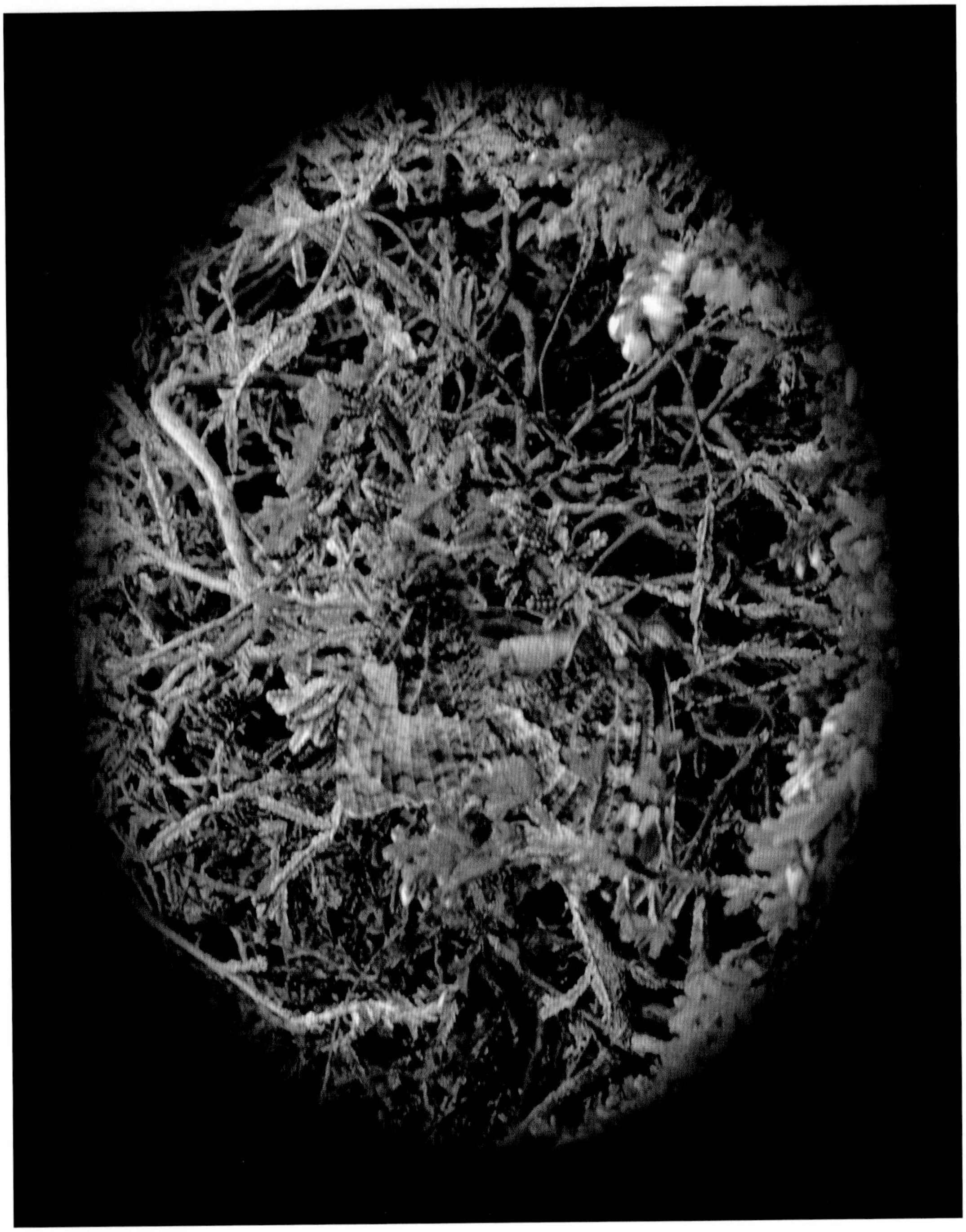

Trees The climax vegetation: carbon storers

How many reasons do we need to appreciate trees? But how often do we se them abused? The rustle of autumn leaves as you walk home from school; white ankle socks turned black with dust, why? Trees filter the air that we breath; more particularly in the summer when the dust rises in the heat.

Mighty Oak

Nature's most important contribution to our country is without question the Oak, Quercus. One might be enough for any school grounds: the initial plan should establish the few places where permanent trees can be planted that can be allowed to grow to maturity. The **ecology** of the Oak can fill reams of paper; it provides a habitat and food for around three hundred little creatures; more than any other species, and this number increases with age. There are a vast number of varieties in this family and many of them hybridize freely. When mature an Oak contains about 1.8 tonnes of CO_2 , equal to 5,400 car miles. As well as surviving the insect onslaught the Oak also provides nest sites for birds; and the older it gets the more holes there will be for Bats and Owls, and its acorns feed numerous small mammals. Its wood has been used for boat and house building and furniture for centuries. It is easy to grow from acorns, but these must be fresh off the tree.

Angle Shades Moth

Of trees for particular uses; Ash is the last into leaf and first to drop its leaves, and this makes it ideal to shade a pond on the south side. If Willows are used near water it is best to use smaller growing kinds like *Salix elaeagnos*. The other choice is **Alder:** this tree has the ability to increase the fertility of the soil with its **nitrogen** fixing bacterial root nodules and as such is known as a pioneer species especially, where there is poor soil.

Yew trees: a very poisonous tree, especially if you are a greedy bullock. However the fruit is very important food for thrushes in winter; the wood is very hard.

Quercus phellos

This is a more unusual but useful tree - a Cork Oak. Much used in the past for wine bottle corks but now superseded by plastic!! In a manufactured form its insulating properties are used for wall and floor coverings.

It is a very unstable tree as a young plant and needs supporting for a few years. Although it is native to more southerly countries it is perfectly hardy in Britain and can be seen at approximately 30 foot high in Wales. This 'fun' one is in Plymouth where it has fallen over but is still living.

In contrast to the Oaks, the Mulberry, of eastern origin, belongs to a small Family: the fruit of the black form in particular, is sweet and extremely juicy. However the white form is the one used for silk worms in China. Like the Cork Oak the Black Mulberry is unstable on its roots, creating often quite grotesque, but fun shapes. Both kinds need to be planted young to get their roots established.

So many subjects can be covered just by accommodating a few choice trees.

Morus alba: the white mulberry; the black form is best for fruit. What a fun shaped tree this weeping form provides.

An **Arboretum** could be in the long term plan, if space is available.

Scots Pine group showing their winter 'bloom' caused by resin that protects many pine trees from the cold in winter.

Scots Pine is our only native pine and is a beautiful tree when mature. Quite easy to grow from seed.

Conifers are hosts to very **specialised** insects. They are not very tasty but here we have a mob of Pine Saw-Fly Moth caterpillars tucking in. As long as they don't eat the bud as well it won't kill the branch. The oak in contrast has huge numbers of insects to contend with.

Birch trees have soft wood which means they are not generally longlived; in landscaping, because of this the native Silver Birch, Betula pendula *is used as a nurse tree for interplanting with hardwood trees.*

Ash flowerhead with distinctive flattened joints.

Birch is quite a large family of which many have very decorative bark. They can be used for fun designs; there usefulness to wildlife is limited although they do harbour aphids and some caterpillars. A **multi-trunked** specimen is less vulnerable to vandalism.

PLANTING

To enable a tree to establish it needs:

- planting at the right time of year
- at the right depth in good non compacted soil
- with the right watering regime for a year
- with the right stabiliser at the right height
- with compost mulch and or old carpet around its base

Willows

For Willows think cricket bats; baskets; water; aspirin and many other uses; now for bio fuel. Put a stem in water about February time and it will readily sprout roots. A stem a few inches long stuck in the ground up nearly to the top will soon produce a tree (mice and voles permitting). This growth can then be **coppiced** at what ever height is needed. Bud pruning can be done at an early stage to create what ever shape of tree you need, this just means rubbing off the buds that are not needed for the design or for weaving. coppicing maximises the uptake of carbon

There are a wide variety of kinds and colours. Recommended for craft work are *Salix virminalis* and *S. purpurea* but for coloured stems there are the following: –

S. irrorata – with black stems
S. *alba 'Cardinalis',* – red stemmmed
S. alba var. vitellina 'Britzensis' – with orange stems.
S. *daphnoides* – has a white indumentum;
S. petiolaris, – purple stems
S. hibernica – with bright green stems.

Weaving can use a large quantity of stems so don't underestimate how many trees will be needed. Hazel, also coppiced, is useful for big projects like bird hides and arches.

An old pollarded Willow : a feature of many landscapes where rivers flow slowly. This will have many creatures living in it and will be cut when the stems are long enough.

Jan's willow bird looks a bit bemused by the building sand or is it the plastic? !

Willow; Alder; Hazel and Birch trees all have catkins; they have the male below that sheds its pollen for other females when the wind blows. The Scots Pine also sheds clouds of pollen on a fine morning in spring time. Hazel pollen in February will cause sneezing when the sun is out.

Flowering Herbaceous Plants

An ancient woodland that has been replanted for timber in the past but never cultivated, this allows the understory to grow undisturbed. This is a mixture of our native Bluebells and Allium ursinum, *Wild Garlic also known as Ramsons.* *INSET: Allium Triquetrum (three sided stems) with Speckled Wood butterfly.*

There is no need to define the different categories of herbaceous plants as they should all be regarded as a learning resource that can be added to or changed as lessons progress; whether they are native, wild, or cultivated for their flower power or edible qualities, does not matter. ***Allium triquetrum*** is also completely edible.

Rosebay Willow Herb has a seed that germinates after fire so this will sprout if there has been a bonfire present.

Many ***genera*** *have become variable over time to adapt to different conditions and this may be evident in the ones studied. In the Willow Herb family; the mountain form is very tiny though with long seed pods that elevate its seeds into the wind, whereas the common Rosebay is already tall, up to 1.5 m: they are both plants of poor quality soil.*

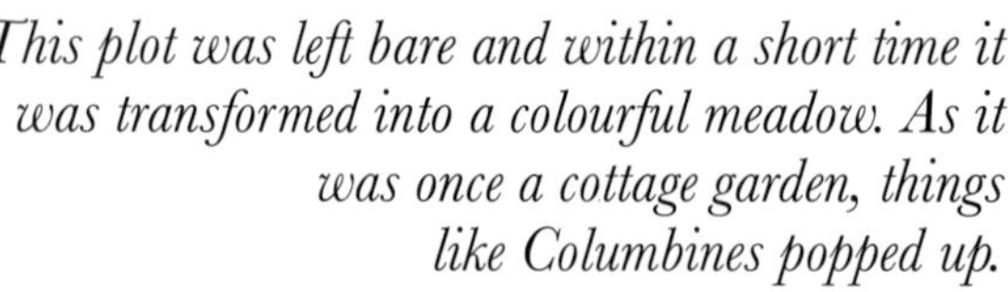

This plot was left bare and within a short time it was transformed into a colourful meadow. As it was once a cottage garden, things like Columbines popped up.

Many plants are useful indicators of soil base material, so it is important to identify and list the species that are already on the site. A trial plot can be left uncut, and another trial plot with turf removed will reveal what is on site within a matter of a few weeks. As a result of this it can be determined if it is worth saving any or all of the existing turf. This will need to be carried out in late spring for best results. In **Nitrogen**-rich soil, a sign of high fertility, the chances are that **Nettles** will sprout up.

Dandelions

Dandelion heaven for hover flies!

The scourge of fussy gardeners, Dandelions are of immense importance as a food plant for grazing animals; for seedheads for small birds, including Goldfinches and Redpolls and for visiting insects to feed on. Seeds persist in the soil, in some cases for a very long time. On the trial plot, as the seedlings come up they can be identified and recorded and then pulled up or moved. In old gardens, seeds freshly exposed to light and air can be very interesting, perhaps Sunflowers, Pansies or Bluebells, but most usual are Foxgloves.

A little light with foxgloved fingers

Some flowers are edible, like Nasturtium and White Waterlily, though not all of them are as tasty as they are attractive. Of course culinary herbs have edible parts, usually leaves, and these should be included in the planting scheme. Because they are often of foreign origin thy could be incorporated into beds designed to show what currently grows in different parts of the world. These plants can form an ongoing study because seeds and rooted plants can be collected as a continuing **project,** also worthy of study is the **interaction** between different plants as noted by experts. One reason for the ground shaping in the original plan is so that there will be slopes and corners and dry and damp places to accommodate different species.

A Sow-thistle, this one has no spines and attracts hoverflies.

Scots Thistle, this one with ferocious spines but lovely flowers and VERY furry leaves.

Thistles: weed or beautiful wild flower?

Seedheads of all thistles are important for birds. *Silybum marianum*, a non-native biennial, is a fine example of a defensive plant; it is completely edible, when minus its prickles; known as the 'Milk Thistle' because of its beneficial use by nursing mothers, it is also shown to be useful in treating liver complaints. Without its spines it would probably have become extinct!

Patterns in nature

Rheum palmatum *is another one to delight children. It is a medicinal member of the Rhubarb family and is quite majestic in Springtime.*

Shrubs and small trees

It might be useful at this point to explain the use of the Latin language for plant names. It was an ancient common language between countries and has the advantage of being very precise for naming plants. Vernacular Common Names, even the standard ones vary between countries; whereas the Latin Botanical Name is constant across boundaries and generally understood. It is a double name; consisting of the generic or group name, always with a capital letter and the specific or individual epithet; now always spelt with a small initial letter, though historically some were capitalised. Latin names are usually italicised or otherwise differentiated from common names – these in ordinary type though usually with capitals.

A tree form of Cotoneaster

Children love a challenge: an introduction to **Latin** is a step in the direction of other language learning as many English words have their origins in Latin or Greek; often via French. Latin was the language of all educated men, particularly physicians who needed to have a sound knowledge of the plants used in medicine, (see: Physic garden in Chelsea). Latin names are usually descriptive; e.g. '*Viscum album*', – meaning simply 'white sticky' – for Mistletoe; but try 'sesquipedalis' or 'sphaerocephalus'; or what about 'quinquevulnerus': easier is 'Saponaria', which is Soapwort, a lovely pink flower sometimes seen along old lanes or in old gardens, whose latex acts as a detergent. Anything with 'officinalis', meaning 'of the pharmacy', in the name, was for medicinal use. Inspiration for a lifetime's learning.

Shrubs are the essential ingredient in any planting. They provide its form and structure; linking its different elements and integrating them into a complete whole. They supply a habitat which gives seclusion, shelter and protection for wildlife throughout the seasons in an otherwise **hostile** expanse, protecting it from predators and disturbance, just as a hedge does; with nesting, roosting and display sites for birds. They also provide food for small mammals and invertebrates; from the nectar and pollen of the flowers, from the leaves and bark and from fruits and fallen leaves. These create an additional **habitat** for small mammals and others and supply the organic matter and nutrients which drive the soils recycling system. This combines the activity of animals; earthworms; fungi and bacteria to eventually release the mineral salts needed by plants for growth. Some soil bacteria also fix and make available for plant needs, some of the abundant, but otherwise inaccessible, nitrogen in the air. They are often greatly assisted in this by further nitrogen-fixing bacteria, which are present in root nodules on many leguminous plants.

Rosmarinus officinalis (Prostratus Group) Prostrate Rosemary

Shrubs vary greatly in character, appearance and habit; from large stout-wooded plants such as many Viburnums, to very small, completely prostrate or woody-cushioned kinds. The dwarfest kinds are generally adapted to more extreme conditions in the Arctic or Mediterranean. For instance a survivor in the Scottish Highlands and Arctic is the Least Willow which has its stems at-or-below ground level with only its leaves above during the brief summer.

A large genus such as Cotoneaster can encompass the whole range and has a member that will fit any situation, right up to 3 meters high. This is probably the most valuable group of all for furnishing school grounds as it is easily grown and easily managed, usually with the bonus of a striking display of autumn leaf colour and, for a short while, berries.

Holly and Ivy growing together. Half an hour later some migrating Redwings had devoured these berries before it snowed. Then the Ivy will ripen, the berries available when it snows next time.

In Britain, Cotoneaster in the wild is only represented by a single very rare species, but it is a large genus with a wide range of form from creeping mats to low dense mounds, to larger dense-twigged bushes, to more open shrubs and on to small bushy trees: all have insect friendly flowers and berries for birds in winter; smaller berries are taken first and larger ones later.
Note: In the 'New Flora of the British Isles' (3rd Edition) by Clive Stace, there is an excellent Botanical key to many species, including introduced, of this complex genus.

Shrubs may be static or may spread by rooting or creeping stems or by rhizomes, as in Rose of Sharon, *Hypericum calycinum*; sucker from the roots, as with Raspberry; or tip layer their long stems as happens very successfully in brambles. Clearly such plants need watching.

In contrast to most hardy trees, many broadleaved shrubs are evergreen. Bold foliaged, sparsely leaved and branched evergreens such as Cherry Laurel and large-leaved Rhododendrons which are of relatively little value except for shelter in Winter, but smaller-leaved, denser, more intricately branched kinds can be of considerable value to wildlife.

Holly and Oak trees once established, can tolerate an Ivy growing with them for many decades.

Ivy flower and fruit

Evergreen foliage is shed after 2-3 years; usually in late spring and is sometimes troublesome at this time; particularly so with Holly and the large-growing Holm Oak. The harder evergreen foliage decays much more slowly than deciduous leaves and if unmixed can build up a thick layer which is insulating, dry, sterile and is therefore inhibiting of the recycling process. Softer deciduous foliage is shed at a more useful time of year and if used as a mulch enters recycling more readily.

Large stronger shrubs have a range of branches which supply birds with surveillance sites and perches for display and song when establishing territorial rights. Intricately branched, small-leaved shrubs many spiny or spiny leaved kinds provide an even greater variety of niche habitats with shelter for fledglings, and feeding sites. Kinds of Berberis are very good providers for birds, including their berries of different colours. It is a large family ranging from dwarf slow growing to 2 meters high; some have defensive thorns on the stems and some have defensive little spines on their evergreen leaves. **Chemistry** is a prime subject for using plants: a dye can be made from the roots of the Berberis family, they have a remarkable yellow sap in the roots and wood. Some have showy flowers in spring; *Berberis darwinii* has very showy bright orange flowers followed by glaucous blue berries, beloved of thrushes.

Berberis vulgaris*: The berries are edible: this shows the growth habit on a bush a meter high, a very hardy plant.*

Mahonia Lomarifolia *flowers*

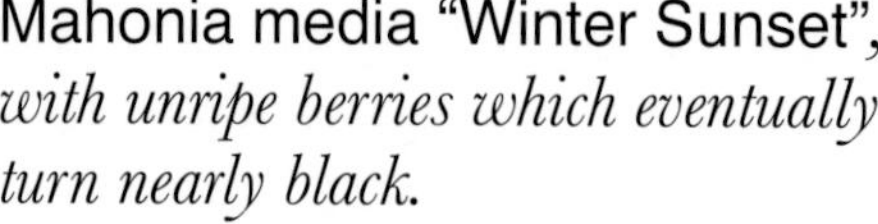

Mahonia media "Winter Sunset", *with unripe berries which eventually turn nearly black.*

The genus Mahonia is closely related to Berberis but the yellow flowers, are in long stiff panicles on erect plants that attract bees in the colder winter months, when there is not much for them to stock up on nectar if they awake during warmer spells, as they sometimes do. Mahonia is easy to look after: these winter flowering kinds are best controlled by allowing them to grow large for several years and then cutting, in alternate years, some of the stems hard down into the old wood and then allowing them to grow again more densely.

In comparison with the above; shrubs like Hydrangeas, except for the climbing form, are not robust enough for the school environs. Lavender; Sage; **Cistus** and Rosemary are amongst these and loved by Bumble Bees, but as these small growing kinds can withstand harsh conditions weather-wise these latter can be given a home on a roof garden.

These are Lavender kinds that have long flower stems which are loved by all kinds of bees and need planting in full sun.

Deciduous, scented, Honeysuckle flowers in January

Gelder rose, not actually a rose: it is *Viburnam opulus*

Sorbus matsumarana

Rosa rugosa "Hansa"

A Mistle Thrush has been enjoying the seeds out of this rose hip belonging to R.rugosa 'Hansa' a tough, easy-to-manage plant. Not many creatures can cope with Rose seeds because they are encased in hairs.

All rose hips are rich in valuable vitamin C.

Roses can be planted within other shrubs if you need to keep them out of direct contact with people. If there is a large old deciduous tree already available there are some suitable climbing roses that will climb to the top of them; some are covered in small hips in winter. All roses attract insects and aphids for the birds. This is the main food source for the chicks of many kinds, when they are first hatched.

If these easy roses are used there will be little or no pruning to be done - this is only for the Hybrid Teas used for bedding displays. Shrub roses like *R.moyesii* are easy to grow and require no pruning.

This is a very artistic rose, R.'Mutabilis', *one of many Chinese Species Roses that has hardly any thorns but is somewhat rangy in habit.*

Rosaceae is a diverse family, from herbaceous sorts up to small trees; it covers Brambles; Raspberries; Sloe; Plum; Cherry; Sorbus, including Rowan; Hawthorn and Cotoneaster; all of which can be usefully represented in school grounds. The one that can be represented by a cultivated form rather than a wild one is the Crab Apple; using the upright growing ones like Malus John Downie or Golden Hornet which produce fruit for making jelly preserve, of an excellent flavour and colour.

Rosa Moyesii an easy shrub rose about 2 meters high.

Cotinus Art in Nature!

Malus Golden Hornet a crab for making jelly preserve.

Crataegus: has haws closely resembling small apples; this is one of the many varieties there are.

Other useful shrubs:

–Elder: for its flowers and fruit; there is a cut and purple leaved "Black Lace" with black berries.

–Guelder Rose: native and introduced kinds;

–*Cornus sanguineus*;

–Buckthorn: two kinds, and the unrelated Sea Buckthorn, which has orange berries which are full of vitamin C,

–Double Gorse: usefully this does not seed down, as it lacks reproductive organs.

–Wild roses: *R.canina* and *R.arvensis*; these in the hedgerow.

–Spindle: the native one is tall and easy.

Of the Dogwoods: Some forms like the non-native, *Cornus capitata*, do provide large edible but tasteless fruits that only Blackbirds seem to like, but the other members of the family are grown for their coloured stems, red, green or yellow in winter. For this they need to be cut back to ground annually.

Pruning

Care must be taken that the all-too-frequent excessive cutting back should be avoided; the supermarket trim is very much what is NOT needed. Most can take an annual cutting back of old and some weak wood but rarely require that comprehensive cutting out of wood older than one year. Correct timing is all important as, for instance pruning a cherry tree anytime except immediately after flowering otherwise it will succumb to Silver Leaf disease and die.

Late flowering shrubs that flower on new growth are pruned in spring, after the worst weather and then the older wood only. The Dogwoods, **Cornus** that are grown for their coloured stems are cut hard back to ground level each year, this has the effect of weakening the plant so it is better to adopt a 2-yearly system; preferably cutting half the stems each year, so that a continuous and more natural structure is maintained. In consequence of the last Ice Age, there are surprisingly few kinds of woody plants and trees native to Britain and apart from the Heather family, also good for roof gardens, there are hardly any low bushy ones.

Vegetables

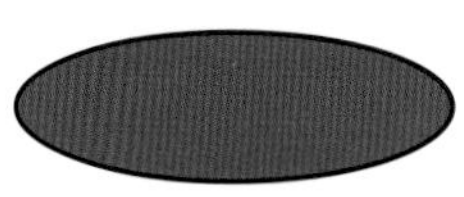

Do children like Cabbage? Probably not. Why not? Probably because it has been presented to them badly, sadly and over cooked. So unless you can grow them to perfection first, lets avoid them for the time being.

Chard is far more enticing; it is colourful and very good to eat.

Spring Cabbage

Children don't generally like the Brassica family so a gorgeous alternative is coloured Swiss Chard. It is easy to grow and is pleasant to eat provided it is carefully cooked: either the stems can be cooked in a stir-fry, or used as small tender leaves added to salad, or for ease the leaves can be steamed; it has the advantage of cut and come again. There is no shortage of colours as the RHS gave seven cultivars an Award of Merit in 2000. Chard is related to Beetroot and the Purple Leaved Orache seen in the Poppies picture (page 6), and has an interesting history in many parts of the world. Most importantly it is medicinally beneficial and provides a supply of nutrients to the winter diet.

Potatoes come in many guises; the ones we are most familiar with are commercially viable kinds, but there are a great many interesting forms that come in different colours as well as black/purple and red. The best ones to grow at school are First Earlies, depending on the part of the country you are in and how far north: mid-March to mid-April is the time for planting. When they have been purchased in late January or February they should straight away be put in an airy place in open egg boxes to sprout from the tubers before planting.

Exhibition potatoes

Early potatoes do not need spraying for blight if they are lifted in time, but later ones do; though blight-tolerant kinds are now being bred. They must never be planted in the same place each year ; they must be slotted into the rotation system. Compost that is sweet and well rotted can be added to the soil for this crop. It is a good crop for breaking down clay soil that has been reclaimed from old turf, this latter left exposed to frost before planting to kill off wireworms and reduce other pests; the birds will be helpful in this respect. Always buy new stock to avoid disease.

© Alaw Jones Red is for tops!

Potatoes have a fascinating history relating both to man's development and botanically. They produce a poisonous top fruit; very closely related to tomatoes, tobacco, peppers and the ornamental Solanum. Because white potatoes were seen as the most desirable when they were introduced to Britain in the 16th century the less appealing colours were bred out. The reason for this could have been the cooking method of boiling because this ruins the colour completely. The fact is that all potatoes are better cooked by baking them in their skins especially as most of the vitamin content is just below the surface.

The displays below are works of art; the result of the dedication of the many enthusiastic and determined vegetable enthusiasts in this country today. Children can enter these competitions at local and county shows and should be wholeheartedly encouraged to do so.

Yes! there are pink (purple really),cauliflowers in the

© Alaw Jones

© Alaw Jones

Show offs !

Potatoes ready to flower and then they can be lifted with a fork. These are three different kinds.

Shallots: these are more practical to grow than the Spanish Onions as they will appeal to children and will be ready sooner. Spring onions might be handy as they can be grown from seed. There is a Tree Onion that grows little plantlets at the top of its stems!!

Broad beans can be planted to kick start the growing year because they can be planted in pots indoors. Some have scented flowers and some different flower colour, as here. Very young beans a few inches long are excellent to eat cooked as a whole tasty pod. Some can be left to grow on to full size.

Broad Bean flowers; they are sometimes scented too.

Other vegetables could be chosen by the pupils; if Runner Beans are suggested then the tall ones may have to be left to its own devices during school holidays; so preferably the small growing dwarf **French Beans** can be used instead; they are happy in raised beds and come in different colours of flower and pod. There are also climbing forms.

A 'Parsley' bird and her chick. This was her third nest of the season in 2009 and the second to be built in the partly open sided greenhouse.

Fruit

Fruit and vegetable growing is a vast and fascinating subject that can introduce children to Science: Chemistry; Biology; Botany; Human Health; Weather; Geology and many other subjects; including gems of information like the use of fertiliser and manure for improving soil and the fact that **Parsley** takes up Iron from the soil. There is no point in children growing things they do not like eating. If they are to be encouraged to learn how to grow food plants they can be inspired by growing enticing and appetizing subjects. However, if first a lettuce is grown from seed this can lead on to bigger and better kinds of plants.

What a wonderful world it is that there are so many varieties of apples in it!

This is a cider apple.

Apple trees: these are grown on rootstocks, varying in vigour. They need to be selected for the conditions and the size of tree required; so sourcing from a knowledgeable grower is the safest course of action. If the outline plan includes a sensible selection then each new year's pupils can plant one for their year and in time a good orchard will develop that will allow future studies. Each year's pupils will then feel they have some responsibility in the grounds. One to be recommended is **Lord Hindlip**: an apple grown in Hereford since 1896, it is a small useful apple that is in season in about February which for school purposes is a good time to be around. It is extremely hardy and disease resistant. Another useful tree is **Discovery,** which ripens early**.** Apple trees do need a good piece of land with rich or enriched soil. Good preparation of ground for each tree will give best results. This is one part of the plan that should and can be made permanent. Damsons; Greengage; Cherry; Mulberry and a few others could be added in time.

Apples for juicing.

–The large Blenheim Orange comes from a very large growing tree. One to plant for posterity!

All the main fruit trees are deciduous, that is, the leaves only last for a single growing season, falling off the trees every autumn. Towards the end of summer the leaf cells become less active and the starch granules in them transform into sugar which makes its way down to the roots where it is reconverted into starch for storage. The leaves have been busy "extracting" the carbon from the air and storing it in the tree ready to supply the new fruiting buds for the following Spring. There are different kinds of fruit that will suit different places but they all rely on frost-free slopes to avoid damage to the spring flowers and most need other kinds to pollinate them. When the fruit is ready it can be pressed for the juice as our local fruit grower does with his mobile press, a demonstration and tasting session may be possible. Fermentation is a chemistry lesson!

JUICE PRESSING

The washed windfall apples are put in a jute sack lined tub with a collection tray underneath it, a lid is then put over it and then the screw handle on top is tightened by one or two people. In the case of a large press this used to be done by a pony. One can assume the pony would then help to eat the remains!

The juice is immediately ready for drinking or for bottling temporarily.

Apple tree pruning is another art that needs to be taught. Most bear their fruit on short lateral 'spurs', but in some the fruit buds are at the tips of the previous years growth, so these stems cannot be shortened without losing the fruit and alternative methods need to be adopted.

The illustration below is of a 'spur': this is the flowering bud on a short stem.

Sampling the results!

Windfall Crab Apples off M. 'John Downie'

Easy and practical, even if the fruit is left on for the Blackbirds, are the Currant bushes. They come in three colours but the Blackcurrants are the most robust growers and can be used to delineate areas or create substantial boundary hedges. Red and White Currants are more restrained growers which can be trained, and can be planted amongst other things for protection. The sooner children learn to identify what is edible and what is not, the better.

These are American blueberries of which there are about 12 kinds available.

Red currants, another bird favorite!

Raspberries are not very practical but other soft fruit like Loganberries_can be grown for interest. Of other fruit, **Vacciniums,** the Blueberries provide a lesson in acid loving species that can easily be grown in large pots, the varieties cover a long season.

Blueberries have terrific autumn colour.

Alpine Strawberries

Especially useful in a raised bed, for obvious reasons, are **Alpine Strawberries;** grown from seed; giving good prolonged fruit production from non-running or slightly running plants which are longer lived and disease resistant. Ordinary Strawberries need much more care for success. Though the domestic varieties can be grown and the runners propagated as an exercise; they can prove troublesome in the school situation as they need quite a lot of attention; but are much more readily grown in hanging baskets.

Climbers

Climbing plants are particularly useful as they take up less space and can be used to cover or disguise buildings and structures, but do check that they won't interfere with overhead cables, gutters or windows. **Grape Vines** are interesting and useful to illustrate or practice pruning techniques because vine pruning can be applied to other plants like Wisteria †. Hops are not directly edible but are useful for attracting Butterflies; especially the tawny, golden 'Comma'(pg 41) which also likes Ribes, some Hydrangeas and Nettles; and there is a modern variety of Hop that is smaller growing than the old fashioned tall one; they are also deciduous.

Wisteria needs to be grown on something robust and secure. not especially useful plant.

Thornless Rose "Zephyrine Drouhin"

The biodiversity value of a tree can be increased by planting a climber to grow up it; only one preferably; this can be Honeysuckle if it is a multi-trunked specimen, but be warned: don't plant **Honeysuckle** with any other climber primarily because it will be extremely troublesome to maintain later.

If an old tree is available then plant a climbing rose up it; choose one with the appropriate ultimate-size compatibility (anything from 3m to 9m). To grow up and over a high wall there is a very fine thornless form called the '**Banksian Rose**'. Wild Dog Rose and others will go into small trees and through hedges, in this way roses greatly increase the value for birds.

Banksian Rose at Kew Gardens, London

† One kind of Wisteria grows clockwise another grows anti-clockwise, why?

If Ivy is already upon the tree and is not evidently harming the tree then it can be left or pruned. **Ivy,** if it can be used, is a very valuable out-of-season plant for winter nectar, and also excellent bird food. It accommodates large numbers of hibernating insects; provides cover for roosting birds and for nesting sites; also, with age, where it can hang down in long streamers it becomes even more useful to birds.

Cotoneaster horizontalis

Possibly Cotoneaster fits in this section, although some of them are better for tumbling down retaining walls they will also grow up a wall a short way or train upwards. This huge family of plants has a variety of habits in it to fit any space and should be included in any plan, for its flowers for the bees in the Spring and for the most valuable bird-berries in the Winter.

Some climbers for high walls that are robustly built and that will be good bird nesting and insect habitat and food providers are the Climbing Hydrangeas. Other climbers, but NOT Honeysuckle or Clematis montana, can be allowed to grow up them, as they mature.

Comma butterfly; here seen on the true flowers of Hydrangea m. Izu-no-Hana' *(not a climber);*

A must for any school grounds is this climbing **Hydrangea petiolaris** (above) it can be grown up trees or buildings up to many meters high. It is solid and vigorous and will grow up virtually anything with the exception of shiny engineering bricks facing south; it is exceptionally good for bees; this is deciduous and H.seemannii is evergreen. Both are good for nesting sites. Plant it thoughtfully!! The only ones suitable for nectar are the true flowers like the one the Comma butterfly is on, most others are only bracts, the Comma is most fond of the flowers of annual Hops.

Clematis montana

Capable of covering the most unsightly of structures

‡ Choose the pure white or deep pink

Ipomea or Morning Glory is an ideal climber for beginners: it needs starting off indoors in spring and climbs fast up anything: its flowers are a really exciting spectacle about mid morning each day in summer. It is an easy annual.

Ladybird scrum by Bron

Tamus communis, the Black Bryony, grows up into hedges and then as the leaves die down for the winter the ripening berries are left hanging like jewels. They then rely on visiting Mistle Thrushes to feed on and digest its fruit to disperse its seeds and cause them to germinate through being in contact with digestive acids. This will be out of harms way up a thick hedge, but remember it has poisonous berries, this information should be an important lesson. If the only bird that can eat this fruit is the thrush and the plant needs its seeds to be digested and distributed then there is vital mutual benefit.

Tamus communis *showing its leaves shriveling up so that the berries are exposed for the birds to see easily.*

Climbing Honeysuckle also does this.

There is however a winter flowering and deciduous kind (page 30) that flowers before its leaves in winter so that its tiny scented flowers are exposed to attract pollinating insects: these could be night flying moths!

Soil is precious stuff and varies from one part of the world to another depending on the underlying geology. One of the main ingredients in it is decayed or pre digested vegetable matter. This has already used water and minerals from underground and the most important thing to do is recycle it all. We gardeners call it composting. Nature goes through this process all the time without our help; so all we need to do is follow natural rules, though we can speed the process up once we have understood the principles involved. We are only concerned with vegetable matter here, but it needs to be understood that all animal, vegetable and some mineral substances can be included in a commercial situation. Mr Simon van der Slikke told the Fruit Growers Association members, in 2010, that 'one teaspoon of a healthy soil contains no fewer than 100 million bacteria, 2,000 protozoa, 50 nematodes (roundworms) and an equally mind-boggling quantity of fungal mycelium'. If manure is stacked before use, it is important to cover it up to maintain its quality. There has recently been a serious problem with contamination of straw by a chemical called **Aminopyralid** which causes growth defects in vegetables. Animal bedding now includes sawdust and other materials and these can be included with discretion. Compost conserves the soil structure and holds nutrients and moisture.

One of the most easily obtained ingredients to start a compost bin are the leaves off the trees. The council contractors can be contacted about this as long as they are aware that leaves from a reasonably uncontaminated site are needed. It is possible for the leaves to be screeded first; then the leaves should be stacked and then gradually added in thin layers between kitchen and garden waste. Small quantities of shredded paper or cardboard soaked in water are not a problem as long as they are used in moderation thus avoiding excessive printing ink contamination.

These are Japanese Maple leaves; any leaves will do except Sycamore and London Plane; evergreens can be kept separate because they take longer to rot down.

The more of the humus produced by composting that can be added to the soil, the more earthworms will be present. There are many kinds of earthworms, the ones that feature predominantly in the new compost are different from the ones found in turf; some form casts on the soil surface and some don't. Altogether there are 26 kinds native in Britain. There is even an **Earthworm Society** based at the natural History Museum in London.

Earthworm in Camomile plants

Compost is essential for increasing the soil fertility, no matter what the underlying geology is. There will be very few, if any, worms in acid soil and lime may need to be added to the compost for this. Clay soil has very little air in it and will need the most work to make it friable; it also needs to be worked on before hot weather sets in as it dries like concrete; so keeping this soil covered with vegetation or a surface layer of mulch of some organic matter is very important. Sandy soil is fantastic for carrots and easy to manage at any time of year, BUT it drains quickly after rain and the rain leaches the nutrients from it, therefore fibrous compost is very helpful for retaining these nutrients and those that are added before planting. It is useful to get a soil testing kit.

The placing of the **composting bins**, as two are the ideal, should be given careful consideration. Ease of access to them is important if people are to be encouraged to contribute material. If school kitchen staff can be involved, then a bin placed where it is as convenient as possible, is essential. There are many ready made bins or tumbling machines, which speed the process up, on the market, but a double holder made of wood or brick will do; if a bottomless old dustbin is used it must have strong wire mesh (weldmesh from a builders' or farmers' suppliers) put underneath to prevent unwanted visitors. Bulk vegetable matter is rotted down by the heat generated in itself. This does not require worms; but a slow composter, as above, does; so a layer of fertile soil will start this process off if the bin is on tarmac. For subsequent heaps, leftovers from the previous one will have worms in them. Leaves and paper based waste need to be incorporated in separated thin layers if they are to break down efficiently. Grass cuttings are best rotted down using a proprietary biological additive. Mainly there is a need to balance the mixture especially between dead material and green material. If there is likely to be an imbalance then keep them separate. Every six months the compost can be emptied and sieved ready for use; the sievings being returned for the next batch.

A small frame with a lid made of twin wall polycarbonate.

NURSERY BEDS

The importance of a small nursery bed or Frame is to provide somewhere to start plants off, prior to being exposed to the full conditions of the open ground or raised beds. It is easier to look after small seedlings in this confined area of a square metre until the weather is suitable for transplanting. These beds can be covered up during adverse weather if necessary. Good clean soil is a prerequisite. If the available soil is on the clayey side it can have sharp sand added for better drainage: available compost that has been well rotted, and preferably sieved, should be added. They are also useful for propagating plant material that has been acquired; hardwood cuttings (preferably taken with a heel) do not need special attention; and for accommodating heeled-in plants in adverse weather, while awaiting fine days for planting into their permanent places. Below a wall in a sheltered place and not in full sun would be ideal.

A mossy ravine where nature is in total control.

WATER

Understanding the ecology of ponds is more than can be fitted into this little effort but a few basic facts are here to help the decision making process easier. Firstly the deeper a pool the better it is for the inhabitants because the greater the depth the cooler it stays in the hot weather and the warmer it remains in the cold weather. One protected deep side and one shallow side with fine gravel and a few boulders will enable birds to bathe and drink and give access to other creatures, and provide a place for children to gain safe access.

Moorhen heading for safety

Dragonfly on Carex pendula with Alchemilla mollis

For a more ambitious pool a long stretch of water is more useful than a conventional round one: it can attract **Swallows** who take water without landing. Interestingly, bats also have this method of drinking while flying along canals and streams. If rainwater is re-directed off the buildings it can come in at one end and go out into a bog garden at the other end. Grey water, from sinks, needs to be filtered through a reed bed (see wwwCAT) and should only be considered if space is available. This will be much appreciated by birds for bathing and drinking and can be located in a shaded or partially shaded place.

Dragonfly heaven!

Still shallow water with marginal plants to lay her eggs in and flowers that attract butterflies and flies for the young ones to eat.

The deeper part, and the sides can be furnished with dominant herbaceous plants and or native sedges, the most useful one being *Carex pendula*, this can be moved around and also seeds freely without being a nuisance; used together with *Salix elaeagnos* to deter pedestrian use in this area; an essential chestnut paling fence here would soon become covered and hidden by vegetation. This is one place where it would be wise to restrict the number of species and only use native material. The local Naturalist's Trust will be able to advise about the local flora as it varies from county to county; some counties have a special **County Flora** book published.

Carex pendula *and* Alchemilla mollis; *two easy plants.*

Broad Bodied Chaser Dragonfly: well disguised

A shallow graded-depth pool can be located on a shed roof.

The small town garden this roof pond is located in attracts over 23 kinds of birds throughout the year.

Bath time for Blue Tit; this in the Winter time. The pebble is warmed up indoors and put in the water to thaw it. for drinking.

Courtyard space

This design is purely decorative and designed to be observed from inside the building. There is no attempt to attract wildlife into it; in fact the opposite was intended because the space is narrow and has to be kept scrupulously clean, especially the water, otherwise it would be very untidy and difficult to manage.

The alternative:
A space for wildlife could be designed for observation only, not to be trampled through, but very visible through one way glass. However, if the space was bigger and had more than one blank wall around it, a smaller pool would suffice and completely different plants put in it, then wildlife could be encouraged. This would of course involve a much more rigorous maintenance program and an acceptance that it would not be quite so tidy.

Avoid placing a pond too near to large-leaved trees because of the leaves and the roots. However a small-leaved tree at some distance and placed to the south will give some useful shade at midday during mid summer. The temptation to plant larger Willows must be resisted near a small pond; although aesthetically desirable they have an enormous uptake of moisture during the growing season. There are smaller kinds in 'Hillier's Manual of Trees and Shrubs' and one that is extremely decorative is *Salix lanata*, with large catkins. If there is space for one, a small island, out of reach of predators, is useful as a retreat for wildlife; it can be a floating raft anchored with a stone or to a post. Alder wood is useful for this job. On a flat or low site, do consider the overflow carefully: a sump dug nearby and filled with rubble, then covered with the path surface or turf, will serve as an emergency overflow and then another small overflow can go to a boggy site; this can be dug to the same pattern as the main pond with a shallow place for seeing things in the water. Hand lenses are valuable and access to a **microscope** is highly desirable.

Being able to see fine detail on butterfly wings or the scales and hairs on leaves can capture the attention and is useful for identification.

Water butts on the down-pipes from the roof are an obvious source of water but children can be encouraged to design ways of distributing it around the site and maybe end up with it in a pond or bog garden. Open water is not absolutely necessary and if not looked after can become a burden. Half-sunken water tubs, which can ultimately be moved around, are quite enough for frogs and little creatures. Birds mainly need a shallow bathing bowl; if the tub is big enough a concrete bird bath stood in the middle provides a shallow pool with shelter under the rim, it needs to be level with the surface of the water.

Nuphar luteum *the native Yellow Waterlily is named Brandy Bottle because of its bottle shaped seed pod (with Bog Bean).*

Bronze Fennel *a herb that is easy to grow and very ornamental as well as edible.*

Gone swimming!!?

Structures

There are endless opportunities for allowing children to get involved with building things; it is very natural to want to build dens of some sort. Using any number of natural materials their imagination can be stretched. Obviously a degree of common sense is involved in the design of any structure and only by early experimentation can the limitations of materials be learnt. The fact is though, that if the element of danger is removed then the ability of children to sense danger is also removed thus causing them to be vulnerable to it. Children need to learn from their environment by being involved in it, not totally protected from it. They can learn practical skills through playing with pieces of timber and tarpaulins and a few bricks or stones.

A structure can ultimately be built over or around an **amphitheatre** provided one was included in the original design. as part of the ground shaping. An open or covered arbour may be built of wood; willow; wire or a combination. A fairly solid framework can be re-covered annually with bio-degradable material every other year; local crafts can be studied for ideas, for example some have thatched roofs and in country districts reeds used to be available. a base of brick or stone could be used as a foundation for the bales if it is designed for longer term use.

Straw bale shelter by Reddy's

The imagination really can be let loose with the straw bale method of creating a fantastic play or lesson enclosure. The structure can be used as it is for one year; the following year holes can be made along the top and edible plants can be inserted in the holes and fed with liquid fertiliser which will produce a crop. Plants to use could be marrows; melons; beans; tomatoes; strawberries and many other artistic mixtures. By the end of the year the insides of the bales should have become most useful compost and can be transfered to the vegetable plots. Then there will be an opportunity for the next intake of pupils to repeat the building exercise. A great mud-making project.

With some preliminary study of ancient building methods beforehand the base could be in stone for a large building, or historic methods of roundhouse construction could be looked at. It is most useful to think small so that it can be built fairly quickly to keep the children's attention, alternatively groups can be formed to do different designs. In some areas hillside houses were built into the slope of a hill; this is where a bank will be useful. If turf is going to be lifted for a planting area it can be staked tidily upside down in whatever shape is needed; this can be topped off with some turf right-side-up to be allowed to grow again; this is a very quick way of creating interesting contours. It could turn into a fun way of creating a realistic natural piece of landscape with hills and valleys, and could incorporate small boulders to illustrate glaciation for a geography lesson. It could even be planted with appropriate species like *Pinus mugo* or *Pinus aristata* (this a montane tree recorded at 5,000 years old); the interesting fact about this very hardy plant is that in its native habitat it becomes white with a coating of resin extruded to protect it from the freezing conditions.

A demonstration building with a **green roof** with wild flowers on top is easy. A rubber liner used over insulation blocks and made ten to thirty centimetres deep will provide a focus point for birds on top of any available shed. An incorporated water bowl would be useful, though it may dry up in summer.

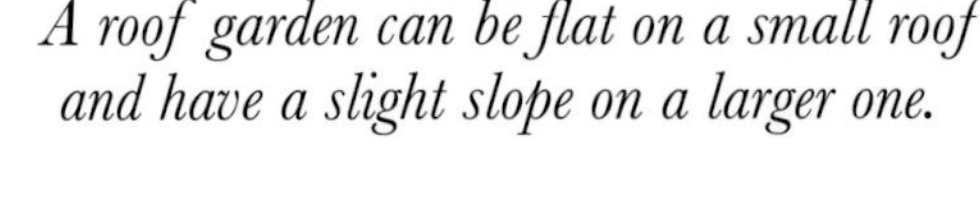

A roof garden can be flat on a small roof and have a slight slope on a larger one.

A strong arch in Glyn's garden made of Hazel wood bent when green or dried and then soaked in water before use.

Enclosures for animals would have been made by an earth bank, with a palisade made of spikes of wood, stuck into the top. To recreate this, chestnut-paling fence poles without their usual wire work can come in handy; they can be used in many imaginative ways. Using a bank also deflects strong wind over a site, and it does not need to be very high to achieve the desired effect; while upright walls and fences cause turbulence beyond them, as previously mentioned.

Willow is the easiest and most practical material for using initially; as the advantage of this method is that everyone can join in at once. If some thought can go into the design beforehand the imagination can be stretched with the use of coloured wood from shrubs such as **Cornus**. Hazel wood can be used for foundation uprights. Willow can be used 'in the green' for this but it will throw new shoots and sprout again when stuck in the ground, even the wrong way up!

If weaving is anticipated, a useful plant is the Cornus family, one of which is native. They can be coppiced regularly to provide a yearly supply. Some of the best are: *C. alba 'Sibirica'* (red); *C. alba 'Kesselringii'* (black); *C. stolonifera 'Flaviramea'* (yellow). They are easily propagated from cuttings, after a few years old plants can be re-propagated and given a layer of compost or leaves and fertiliser if they are to be used for cutting.

Cornus varieties: some are more vigorous than others. These are very attractive in Spring with little Narcissus or daffodils planted under them.

Landscape details

On a flat site it is desirable to introduce shape and contours but on a sloping site there may be a need to look at incorporating change of levels features that are safe and practical. Edges should be flat where different surfaces meet, using concrete slabs or preferably engineering bricks laid flat, as they can be used to form curved edges better(they are frost proof). Railway sleepers, if cleaned of tar, are good for high retaining walls but should be used with caution if they are to be walked across as they can be slippery when wet or frosted. If new wood is used it lasts longer if it is rough sawn and NOT planed smooth.

A path that is built up higher in the centre to create a 'camber' , and lower at the sides will have natural drainage and last longer in good condition than a flat one. There is no reason why a climbing frame could not be built over a path as part of an adventure circuit. Drainage material is better under footpaths built with graded material, as the Romans built roads, so that there is no need for landscape fabric. Footpaths can be used for measuring practice and experimenting with different materials. A little used path can be of grass provided it is designed to be double the width of the mowing blades used by the contractors so that it is economical to cut. Flat brick or slab edge is easier to mow across.

If steps are necessary they should always be built with each riser the same measurement. If there is a problem of space for these they could be taken up sideways across the slope. A handrail can be incorporated on the right hand side. Making everything 'safe' for youngsters does not prepare them for the day when they will be faced with anything not so safe.

Stone steps in a Welsh garden

The freedom to learn the extent of their **capabilities** is important.

Building climbing frames etc. all in one place means that there is great pressure on the one surface, so if they can be incorporated around a planted area it will spread out wear and the surfacing will last a bit longer. A common hazard around play equipment is a low wooden edging, so the use of alternatives should be explored. Consider an edge that also acts as seating; such as large logs: more aesthetically pleasing. A hedge of an easy plant such as *Viburnum tinus* could be used: it needs to be pot-planted as a 50 cm-plus potted specimen. If such a hedge is used a reinforcement, while it is establishing, could be made with some posts and chestnut paling fence along it. This is a very useful kind of barrier in any situation because it is very difficult to vandalize or climb over. An alternative is **Blackcurrant** bushes as these are fairly robust as a hedge.

Chestnut paling comes in a roll joined together with wire. Here the wire has been removed and the poles nailed cross-wise and fixed on top of a wall.

The plant is a fuchsia flowered gooseberry.

Ecology

Ecology is the study of the relationships and interactions of living organisms in an ecosystem. This interplay is basic to the survival of all living things and a study of it can be begun before any groundwork. Studying what is on the site and making a record, both written and photographic will be very useful at the end of the year or term. Everything can be looked at from the kind of soil to the vegetation type and species and any insects as well. A footprint trap of sand or clay can be made to see what can be detected overnight. Anything which is interesting or rated important can be kept, as a cast, as well as recorded. In the new plan a corner might be usefully allocated to **wilderness,** a space for the local flora and fauna community to develop unhindered.

Earth ball in a bed of rotting leaf debris and Polytrichum moss; it is here full of water but when first open and dry releases clouds of spores.

This area can be contrived; it need not be very big as long as it can act as a refuge from feet and disturbance for shy creatures during the day; whatever lives in there will eventually come out and be detected. Fun can be had working out what it will need and how it can be subtly fenced, or otherwise protected. It might have an existing shrub at its centre or it could have one planted; a Hazel, Elderberry or other native bush. Wildlife can be encouraged by including an old fashioned, upturned dustbin or dustbin lid or an old table with bits of wood crammed in under it. A specially built willow arbour or a large pile of logs will do; they will all serve their purpose.

The better it is put together the longer it will last; it could be a stronger structure using old bricks or stone. Plastic should be avoided because it is not UV protected and will deteriorate rapidly in sunshine and is not environmentally friendly. Positioning this area in line with the boundary will be helpful.

Bees and others

Planning a well mixed planting scheme will provide enough diversity to attract the most creatures; this richness of homes and food supplies will enable the natural, local community to thrive and provide the maximum benefit for learning purposes. There is no need to restrict the scheme to entirely native plants, the addition of introduced species will widen the scope for projects e.g. an *Acer cappadocicum* we had, attracted a leaf cutting bee which was nesting in the eaves of a nearby roof, she did not favour any other plant and could easily be observed, there was a very lacy-leaved tree left, but it did not do it any harm despite being nibbled.

Leaf Cutter Bee on Acer cappadocicum

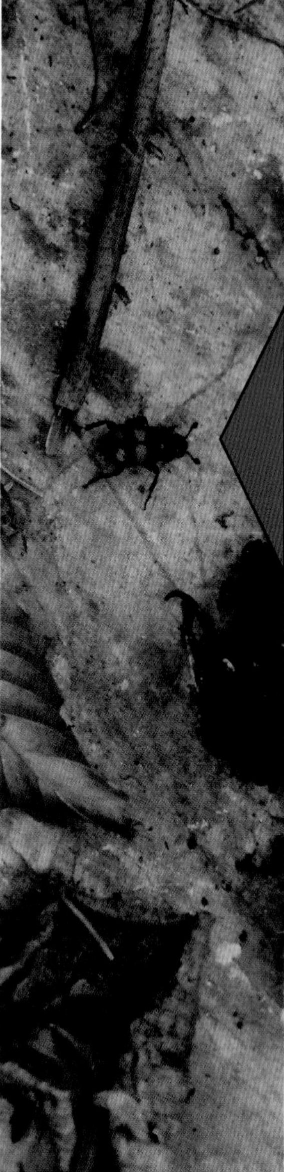

A burying beetle needs an undisturbed place and is rarely seen; this one was trying to bury a mouse that had died in a milk bottle which it could not escape from!

There are more than 200 British species of **bees**, who are all crucial to fertility. They are very important pollinators of the earliest fruit trees to flower. It is especially important to remember that with the onset of a warmer climate many of our native plants will not be able to acclimatise quickly enough to survive and therefore a longer season of flowers can be achieved through the inclusion of plants from other parts of the world. This could be from a colder or warmer climate originally; the natural cross breeding of plants could possibly save a few of the many extinctions that are expected in the not too distant future.

Some Genera [or groups] of plants are very successful in adapting to various climates: prime examples are the Birches and Alders, many of which were recently re-collected from around the world by the late Kenneth Ashburner, of Dartmoor.

At ground level the number of earthworms in a square of soil is an indicator of the fertility of the soil. This can be determined by putting a piece of wet sacking or thick old carpet on the turf for a couple of days and then lifting it to find the results. Again, life is full of surprises: some familiar worms create casts on the surface; but most kinds don't and these include the best ones for compost heaps; while some are too small to see with the naked eye and others are very long. Worms and many insects and especially slugs and snails, masticate dead or sometimes living vegetation which all adds to the soil fertility. Giving the slugs and snails something to eat could keep them away from our seedlings, experimenting can be done: dig a small hole and put different things in it to find out what they like, it can be covered with a slate or roof tile, they will find their way under it by smell. Choice bits of snails are an essential part of a fledgeling thrush's diet, but if the snails have eaten slug bait the chicks will die.

Thrushes anvil

Song Thrush

The Senses

Learning the generic names enables identification to be established more easily in the library or on-line. However even this does not ensure that nature won't trip us up occasionally: the fact that some species have alternate leaf arrangements and others, with very similar leaves, have opposite, is a crucial distinction to be aware of. All the human senses come into play when studying nature - smell; sight; touch and even sound: as when you can hear a solitary wasp gnawing at a piece of wood for its nest, or bamboo crackling as it grows, or the scent of some leaves in the sun. A garden on hill land in Northern England planted with a collection of **Mediterranean Cistus** plants had an amazing variety of Bumble Bees feeding on them.

This Cistus has very sticky leaves

The life cycle of a Pale Tussock Moth

Who would have thought these three pictures were of the same creature?

It pupates in a cocoon in a dry place, in big dry leaves or in crevices in bark, to be able to survive the winter.

It becomes a caterpillar to take advantage of the food available during the growing season and disguises itself to look decidedly inedible to birds.

It hatches out of its silken cocoon and flies away in order to mate and spread its eggs far and wide.

Large Emerald Moth just hatched out under Ivy.

Children's delights!

Healthy soil is full of living organisms, particularly opportunistic fungi and bacteria that break down the organic matter; usually using soil based oxygen which releases nutrients for plant uptake, and also carbon dioxide, which diffuses up and becomes again available for plants. A small proportion of nutrients, such as some nitrate, arrive dissolved in rain. A survival strategy used by the roots of some plants to reach water, is to penetrate to great depths; like the Wild Thyme plant reaching up to one meter, Convulvulus up to two meters and Tamarisk down to thirty meters. There are all sorts of hidden systems under the soil surface where all kinds of weird and wonderful relationships go on between **mycorrhiza** and roots – Mycology being a huge and fascinating subject.

Meadow Wax Cap

Sulphur Tuft

Life is a giant round of feeding forays; the higher "round table" of mammals and birds is inter-connected with the "underground table" of bugs and wriggly things, many microscopic, beneath our feet which is a veritable 'feast on feast'. What we see on the surface is but a tiny fraction of the activity hidden below.

Thyme - with an unfortunate Swallow

The Mole - my landscape architect

Moles who are down more than up, and live on creatures which eat vegetable matter such as earthworms; on the root-eating larvae of various insects; on Mice and sometimes on Lizards and Frogs. Even weaker members of his own species can fall victim to his ravages; while if he exposes himself on the surface he himself becomes food for Owls and other nocturnal hunters. **Moles** are essentially woodland creatures belonging to a food chain which constantly recycles the detritus of plants enabling a healthy life cycle to continue. They are extraordinarily active in the spring when foraging is abandoned, in order to trace shallow tunnels in hot pursuit of a mate. As there are more males than females fierce struggles for possession take place; their love-life and their appetite are insatiable and their presence is an indicator of very healthy soil. Their mounds, full of bug-free soil are ready to be colonized by ripe seeds; an inspection of these will show you what kind of soil is under the ground and the texture of it, also on hilly terrain where the best soil is. They will only forage where there is food, and where there is food there is healthy well drained soil.

Survival

Once an interest in Ecology or Biology is sparked off it can be followed throughout life because they are such vast subjects. Science begins with observation followed by interpretation; learning the value of nature and the medical benefits it provides in so many ways. A well grown and diverse environment is not demanding: in exchange for a little loving care and attention it can be the most valuable path to children's development.

" the more diverse and complex the ecosystem the more stable it is . . . . .the more species there are and the more they interrelate the more stable is their environment. By stability is meant the ability to return to the original position after any change". "A tropical Rain Forest supports innumerable insect species and yet is never devastated by them". *

What can be understood by this is that a monoculture is the opposite in that a single species can readily be wiped out.

On top of the soil – itself shallow – is the very thin green line on which we live. We desperately need to conserve this, and one of the most important ways of doing this is to keep it well planted. Trees are particularly important, where there is space enough for them because they are great recyclers in their own right, they also provide **oxygen** from **photosynthesis** during the day and their role as balancers of the atmosphere should be taken into account. If you observe that the snow melts first where trees are growing you will be witnessing the proof of this. Trees help to stabilize soil erosion and shade fields and roads from hot sun and desiccating winds.

We have been warned: the great urban architect, Le Corbusier believed that,"Man, though qualified by his intellectual capacities and inherent ambition to master the natural world, was in fact, very much a product of it, capable of sharing its rhythm and likely to lose equilibrium if he ignored it".

* from: ' A Blueprint for Survival', in the "Ecologist," January 1972

The trees and everything we rely on depend on the health of the soil, and soil is a complex mix; understanding what is it composed of and how the ecology functions is a lesson about how necessary it is for life. We are the most successful species on earth but also the most destructive.

On building soil:

"Weeds play their part in building soil fertility and in balancing the biological community. As a fundamental principle, weeds should be controlled, not eliminated". –
–Masanoba Fukuoka in the 'One Straw Revolution', (p. 34, 1978)

In rushing forward, we are falling behind - in our haste, we forget to ponder, and relax and see the small things that, taken as a whole, enable life to go on in our shrinking world. The history of gardening over more than two hundred years gives a perspective on the future. Our immediate forefathers were convinced that tidiness was paramount throughout the garden: it began in the vegetable plot and continued into the ornamental garden following viewings of the geometrically designed and highly manicured French and Italian Renaissance gardens on the Grand Tour. It was exemplified by the invention of the lawnmower in 1832, scythes having been used before this. The control over grass was an obsession which relegated flowers to tidy beds borders and pergolas. the next concern was with chemicals and insect killing products. Slug bait (kills nearly as many birds as slugs); mole traps and aphis sprays have been advocated in our gardening press for many long years. Our ancestors thought nothing of using poisons like Arsenate of Lead; Gas Lime; Prussic Acid and other dubious chemicals in the garden.

A manmade landscape can be beautiful and functional at the same time.

The choice is ours!

People frequently had nasty accidents as a result, but the impact on wildlife of all kinds is not recorded; though later, in the 1950's, deaths occurred of all manner of invertebrates, mammals and birds from accumulated DDT originating from widespread spraying and concentrated through the food chain. This eventually led to the product being outlawed.

Perhaps the turning point came after this at the **Rio Earth Summit** in 1992, but then again maybe it didn't. Local Agenda 21 was defined as "Sustainable development which meets the needs of the present without compromising the ability of future generations to meet their own needs", and was a commitment to "development which meets the needs of future generations to live in a way which keeps within the carrying capacity of supporting natural systems". Though we can not suddenly turn the clock back to comply with this commitment we can try to help nature recover from our destructive ways.

On my computer keyboard it is nearly my hand span from 1 to 9, I wonder what the next hand span of years holds? What right have we got to seek out other planets when we are trying our best to ruin the one we have at present? Our future will be determined by our relationship with our planet; to grasp an understanding of why we are us, we need to look back at the Earth's beginnings. We know that the primeval Earth was a molten mass and that many changes occurred before we arrived here, we also know that these processes are ongoing and will not stop. Please teach children to love the planet because it is the only one we have.

END?

Under Spaghetti Junction (Birmingham): one for tomorrows archeologists

APPENDICES

USEFUL BOOKS:

BTCV: "Walling" and "Hedging"

"Concise British Flora in Colour"	by Keble Martin Pub. Ebury Press
"Herbs"	by Roger Philips & Nicky Foy Pub. Pan 1990 ISBN 0 330 30725 8
"One Straw Revolution"	by Masonoba Fukuoka 1978 (out of print but worth seeking)
"Plant Names Simplified"	by Johnson & Smith
"Poisonous Plants & Fungi"	by Marion Cooper & Anthony Johnson Pub. Stationary Office
"Stern's Dictionary of Plant Names for Gardeners"	Pub. Cassell 2002 ISBN 030436469X
"Trees": an inspirational book	by Hugh Johnson ISBN 9781845330552
"Vegetables" (also other useful titles)	by Roger Phillips & Martin Rix Pub.Macmillan ISBN 0 333 62640 0
FRUIT TREE SUPPLIERS: Training & Advice	Frank P. Mathews Ltd Tel. 01584 810 214
Information about fruit trees:	Marcher Apple Network.org

USEFUL WEB SITES:

www.awtc.co.uk The Association of Wildlife Trusts Consultancies

www.bbceducation green classroom; many links

www.bentonite.co.uk for large rolls of clay-based pond lining

www.butterfly-conservation.org

www.britishmycologicalsociety.org.uk for educational resources all Key stages & post 16

www.CAT.org.uk for courses, publications and CPD

www.edenproject Cornwall for educational visits

www.invictagroup.co for teacher resources

www.metoffice.gov.uk "Act on CO_2" Climate change facts.

www.midlandforest.org

www.nationalvegetablesociety.org

www.ourplanet.org renewable energy education

www.seasearch.org.uk Marine Conservation Society

www.severndiybriersjeltd.uk for selection of children's work gloves

www.SirCrispinTickell "The Day After Tomorrow"

www.thegardenmarketplace.co.uk wild flower plugs

www.vigopresses.co.uk everything for fruit pressing

www.wildlifetrusts.org.uk nationwide and includes marine protection

Correct at going to press.

INDEX

GENERAL

BUTTERFLIES:
Comma

Large Skipper

Speckled Wood

Dark Green Fritillary

FUNGI:

Earth Ball

Meadow Wax Cap

Sulphur Tuft

MOTHS:

Angle Shades

Pale Tussock

Large Emerald

Pine Sawfly

PLANTS